Cornerstones of Freedom

The Story of

Jane Addams
and Hull House

Deborah Kent

CP CHILDRENS PRESS®

CHICAGO

Library of Congress Cataloging-in-Publication Data

Jane Addams and Hull House / by Deborah Kent.
    p. cm. — (Cornerstones of freedom)
    Summary: A biography of the social worker who
defended the oppressed, promoted education for the
poor, worked for world peace, and founded Hull House,
a settlement house in the industrial slums of Chicago.
    ISBN 0-516-04852-X
    1. Addams, Jane, 1860-1935—Juvenile
literature. 2. Social workers—United States—
Biography—Juvenile literature. 3. Social reformers—
United States—Biography—Juvenile literature. 4. Hull
House (Chicago, Ill.)—History—Juvenile
literature. 5. Social settlements—Illinois—Chicago—
History—Juvenile liter. [1. Addams, Jane, 1860-
1935. 2. Social workers. 3. Hull House (Chicago, Ill.)
History.] I. Title. II. Series.
HV40.32.A33K46 1992
361.3'092—dc20
[B]   91-378
                                                      C

"One snowy morning . . . I arrived at Hull-House, Chicago, a little before breakfast time, and found there Henry Standing Bear, a Kickapoo Indian, awaiting for the front door to be opened. It was Miss Addams who opened it, holding on her left arm a . . . pudgy baby, belonging to the cook, who was behindhand with breakfast. Miss Addams was a little hindered in her movements by a super energetic kindergarten child, left by its mother while she went to a sweatshop for a bundle of cloaks to be finished. We were welcomed as though we had been invited. We stayed."

Hull House was one of America's first community centers.

So wrote Florence Kelley, describing her introduction in 1891 to a place that would shape her life and career. Anyone who arrived at the doorstep of Hull House could count on welcome and assistance. Jane Addams, its founder, stands out as one of the most dedicated social reformers in American history. For nearly fifty years, she defended the oppressed, promoted education for the poor, and worked tirelessly for world peace. But she is remembered most of all as a good neighbor to the people of the Chicago slum where she made her home.

Jane Addams was born in 1860 in Cedarville, Illinois. She was the youngest of eight children.

Jane Addams's birthplace, Cedarville, Illinois

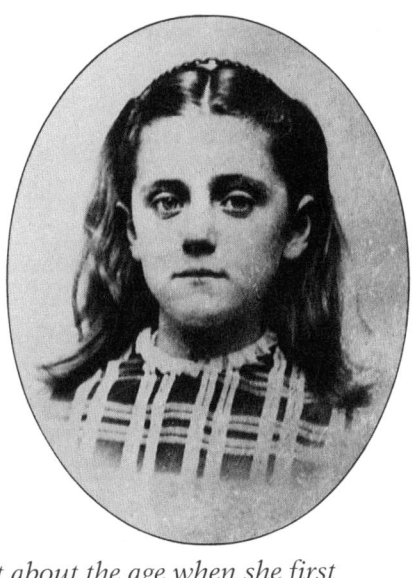

Jane Addams (right), shown here at about the age when she first realized that there were others less fortunate than herself, credited her father (left) with molding her character.

When she was only two years old, her mother died. As Jane grew up, her father was at the center of her life. Years afterward, when the public heaped praise upon her for her good works, Jane Addams always gave her father credit for molding her character.

One day when she was seven years old, Jane asked her father why some of the children in town lived in dirty little houses crowded close together. He explained gently that many people were poor and uneducated, with few opportunities in life. According to her autobiography, Jane decided on the spot that "When I grew up I should of course have a large house, but it would not be built among the other large houses, but right in the midst of horrid little houses like these."

As a child, Jane had an infection that left her with a slightly curved spine. Despite her poor health, she spent endless days exploring the woods near her home, catching snakes, and playing games of pretend. When she was seventeen, she entered nearby Rockford Female Seminary (now Rockford College). The director urged Jane to become a missionary, but the religious life did not appeal to her. She wanted to help people, but was not sure how or where to begin.

After graduating from Rockford, Jane enrolled at the Women's Medical School of Philadelphia. She soon found, however, that she did not like studying dull medical texts. During this time, her old back trouble flared up again. After a few months, she left medical school.

In the late 1800s, few careers were open to women. In those days, most people thought that it wasn't proper for a woman to hold a job; that a woman's place was at home, raising children. Often, a girl would flourish in college, only to return home after graduation, unable to find a way to put her education to practical use. Like hundreds of other educated young women, Jane Addams found herself without useful work to do. As she waded through the empty days, she grew more and more depressed. Finally, her doctor prescribed a two-year trip to Europe to restore his wilting patient to health and happiness.

Jane explored galleries, palaces, and cathedrals, absorbing the culture of the Old World. One Saturday evening, she visited a fruit-and-vegetable auction in a poor, run-down London neighborhood. Half-starved men and women crowded the pavement, bidding fiercely for bruised and decaying produce. Jane was shocked when one man bought a battered cabbage and sat on the curb to devour it, raw and unwashed as it was. As she later wrote in her autobiography, "The final impression was of . . . myriads of hands, empty, pathetic, nerveless and work-worn, clutching forward for food which was already unfit to eat."

While in Europe, Jane witnessed the poverty of London's East End, portrayed here in a nineteenth-century engraving of people grabbing for tickets to a soup kitchen.

After visiting London's Toynbee Hall (right), Jane (left) decided to establish a similar settlement house in Chicago.

On a second trip to Europe, Jane toured Toynbee Hall, an experimental project in a poverty-ridden section of London. Educated young men who moved into Toynbee Hall offered literacy classes, art lessons, and other activities to the people of the neighborhood. Because the men did not merely visit the area, but actually settled in the neighborhood to offer their help, Toynbee Hall was called a settlement house. By the time she returned to Illinois, Jane Addams had decided to establish a settlement house of her own in the industrial slums of Chicago.

During the summer of 1889, Jane visited the city's churches, civic organizations, and wealthy citizens, winning generous support for the project. She also searched for a house that would be suitable for her plans—a large house built "in the midst of horrid little houses." She found it at last, a sturdy brick mansion on Halsted Street on the city's industrial Near West Side. When built forty years earlier, it had been located in Chicago's outskirts. Now the city had engulfed it, and it was surrounded by noisy, dirty tenements. Because the original owner's name was Charles Hull, the mansion came to be known as Hull House.

The reception room at Hull House

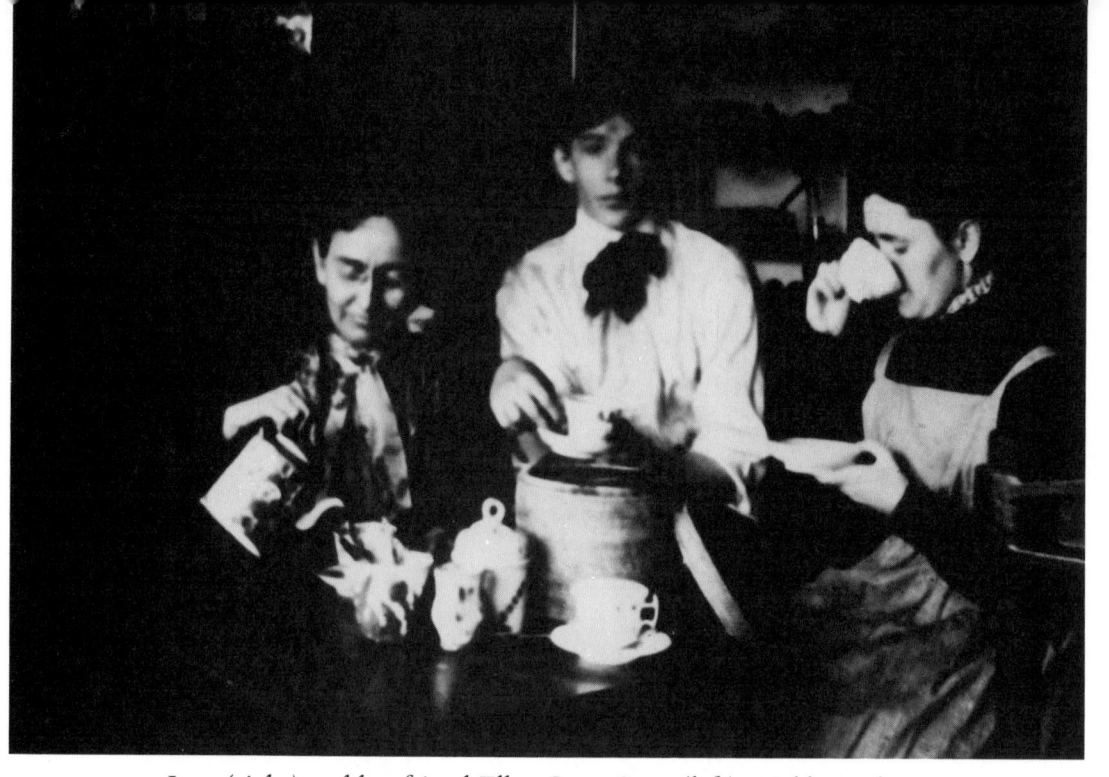

Jane (right) and her friend Ellen Gates Starr (left) quickly made Hull House their home.

With Ellen Gates Starr, a friend from Rockford Seminary who joined her in the settlement project, Jane Addams rented the second floor of Hull House and a large reception room on the main floor. The owner eventually donated the whole building, free of charge.

Friends warned Jane and Ellen that they would be robbed, that they would abandon the venture within a few weeks. But the two young women could hardly wait to get started. Lovingly, they scrubbed and swept, hung curtains, and put their favorite pictures on the walls. Jane later wrote, "Probably no young matron ever placed her own things in her own house with more pleasure than that with which we furnished Hull House."

In the late 1800s, Chicago was a city where great wealth (left) and desperate poverty (right) existed side by side.

It is little wonder that some of Jane Addams's friends were horrified. In 1889, Chicago was a city in which two vastly different worlds existed side by side. On one hand, Chicago was the domain of the privileged and well-to-do; a landscape of galleries, theaters, and elegant hotels. But Chicago had a darker side as well. Writer Lincoln Steffens described it as "first in violence, deepest in dirt, loud, lawless, unlovely, ill-smelling, . . . the teeming tough among cities." Jane Addams was rejecting a life of comfort to settle in one of Chicago's most infamous sections.

Along with a housekeeper named Mary Keyser, Jane Addams and Ellen Starr moved into Hull House on September 18, 1889. They had no

The Hull House neighborhood

definite program in mind. Jane had, however,
developed a philosophy toward the work they
were about to begin. She reasoned that in a
close-knit community, neighbors celebrated each
other's triumphs, helped each other through hard
times, and shared each other's grief. She and
Ellen would try to be good neighbors to the
people who lived near Hull House. They would
care for children, visit the sick, and help prepare
the dead for burial. In addition, they would
encourage other young women and men to live at
the settlement house and bring their talents and
knowledge to the community. Hull House would
not only serve the impoverished neighborhood in

In the late 1800s, many immigrants worked in hot, overcrowded factories known as sweatshops.

which it stood. It would also teach the privileged about the needs and joys that all people have in common. Furthermore, it would provide aimless young people with a fresh new purpose in life.

Most of the people who lived in the crowded neighborhood around Hull House were recent arrivals from southern and eastern Europe. They had fled poverty or political oppression in Italy, Greece, Ireland, southern Germany, or Russia to seek a better life in America. Instead, they found endless toil in factories that were so hot and airless they came to be called sweatshops. The immigrants' wages were sometimes as low as forty cents a day. Moreover, they had to face the prejudice of more-established Americans.

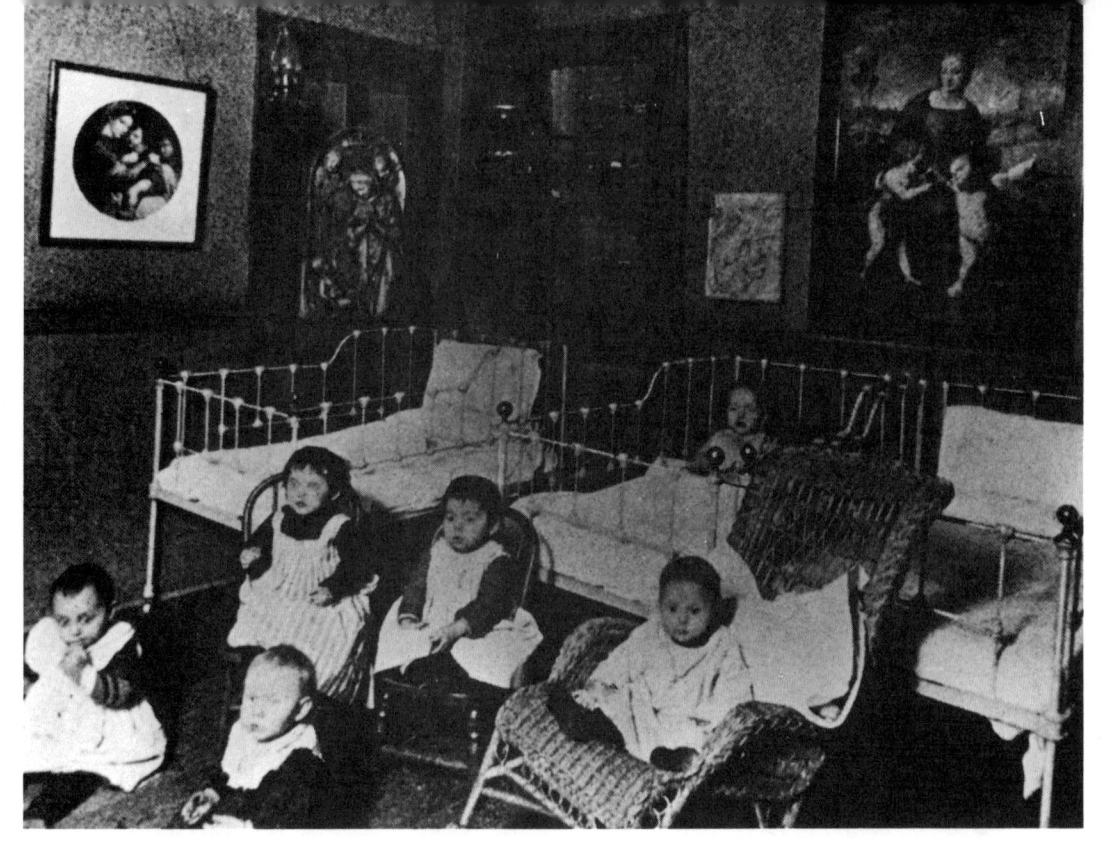

The Hull House day nursery

Businessmen and public officials often claimed that the newcomers were poor because they were inferior.

Some neighbors watched with suspicion as the crisply clean, well-dressed young women moved into Hull House. Others were openly curious. When Jane and Ellen sat on their front stoop, smiling at passersby, people began to stop and say hello. One morning, a harried young mother asked if the women could care for her baby while she ran an errand. Within a week, they were tending several children every day.

In the evenings, Jane and Ellen invited their neighbors to readings from Shakespeare and the

A Hull House party featuring German music and dancing

Greek classics. They lent out books and paintings. Sometimes they hosted parties featuring Italian cuisine or German music. Some people were drawn to Hull House by specific activities. Others merely hungered for a place where they could relax, free from the cares of daily life. Years later, one man recalled, "It was the only house I had ever been in where books and magazines just lay around as if there were plenty of them in the world."

Over and over again, Jane Addams was shocked by the isolation of her immigrant neighbors. Few had ever visited a museum, a library, or even a city park. Their lives were restricted to small, crowded apartments and the stifling factories where they worked twelve or fourteen hours a day. Once, at a Hull House party, a guest asked how the roses on the table were still so fresh after coming all the way from Italy. When Jane insisted she had bought the roses right in Chicago, the woman shook her head in disbelief. In six years, she had never seen roses in America.

As Jane Addams had hoped, idealistic young women and men flocked to Hull House. Each brought a unique set of interests and talents to the community. Mary Rozet Smith was a devoted supporter of all Hull House activities and became Jane's lifelong companion. Julia Lathrop worked

Mary Rozet Smith (left) and Julia Lathrop (right)

The Hull House residents formed a close-knit family.

tirelessly to improve conditions for children, and helped to establish Chicago's first juvenile court. Dr. Alice Hamilton was one of the first Americans to recognize lead poisoning and cocaine use as threats to public health. Florence Kelley investigated the shameful conditions at the sweatshops. She fought for safety standards on the job and for more humane working hours.

United by their admiration for Jane Addams, the Hull House residents formed a close-knit family. They went for hikes and bicycle trips together, and sometimes sat around the dining-room table, talking late into the night. They did not always agree on the best methods to bring about social change. But all were deeply touched by the suffering they witnessed every day, and all were committed to helping others in whatever ways they could.

Jane Addams always felt that her experience at Hull House deepened her insight into the human condition. On one occasion, for example, it took a tragedy to make her rethink her attitudes. An unemployed shipping clerk arrived at the door and asked for money to buy food for his family. Jane told him that workers were needed to dig a drainage canal nearby. She urged him to look for work anywhere he could before seeking a handout. The young man said that he had never been able to endure outdoor work during the winter, but he went away and took a job on the canal. Within two days, he came down with pneumonia, and a week later, he was dead. In her autobiography, Jane wrote, "I cannot see [his two children] without a bitter consciousness that it was at their expense I learned that life cannot be administered by definite rules and regulations."

Hull House provided books and magazines for children to read.

Hull House served thousands of people in thousands of ways every year. Children came to play; their parents studied English; their grandparents taught songs and folk dances from the old country. Jane Addams and the other residents offered relaxation and fun, cultural enrichment, friendship, and hope to the struggling families of industrial Chicago.

The cultural activities offered at Hull House included art classes, which produced some fine artwork (top left); a theater group, shown here getting ready for a performance (top right); and get-togethers in which Hull House neighbors preserved the crafts of their native lands (bottom).

It was soon clear, however, that neighborly kindness was not enough. How could Hull House make a difference when children as young as six worked ten- and twelve-hour days in the sweatshops? What good were art classes when young people were dying of typhoid and tuberculosis? The settlement needed to become politically active. The Hull House group began working for state laws to regulate child labor. Eventually, Julia Lathrop and some of the other residents went to Washington, D.C., and lobbied for reforms on the national level. But Jane Addams's first brush with political action occurred close to home.

A woman and five children lived in this one-room dwelling near Hull House.

Children playing in a garbage-strewn alley near Hull House

In warm weather, the streets around Hull House reeked with the stench of garbage. Large wooden refuse bins overflowed onto the pavement. If a horse fell dead in the midst of the day's work, its body rotted where it lay. Jane Addams protested to City Hall that the garbage collectors were not carrying out their duties. At first she tried to change the way sanitation workers were hired and monitored, but her efforts met with failure. Finally, in 1895, she herself was appointed garbage inspector of Chicago's Nineteenth Ward, at a salary of one thousand dollars a year. It was the only paid position she ever held in her life.

Jane Addams and the Hull House group fought to end child labor (right).

During the early years, journalists applauded Hull House's efforts on behalf of the poor. Contributions flowed in from all over the nation. Yet when Jane Addams and the other residents began fighting to end child labor and establish an eight-hour workday, many influential people began to view them with suspicion. Factory owners shouted that they were a bunch of troublemakers who wanted to keep honest businessmen from earning a profit. The activities of the Hull House group, said some, ran counter to everything America stood for.

Years later, Jane Addams recalled her first decade at Hull House as "a blur of exhaustion." Always a new crisis demanded her attention;

always there were letters to write, funds to raise, legislators to persuade. In 1899, a visitor wrote, "She runs over to Mrs. Jones, . . . up to Mrs. Kenyon, off with Mrs. Haldeman, down to inquiring strangers, and in and out and around about to Italian fiestas, . . . marriages, rows between scabs and unions, etc., etc., etc., until my head spins and I sink exhausted."

Through the early years of the twentieth century, Jane Addams's influence broadened. She lectured on college campuses and spoke to civic organizations. She explained her social theories in a series of books: *Democracy and Social Ethics*, *The Spirit of Youth and the City Streets*, and *Newer Ideals of Peace*. In 1910, she published her autobiography, *Twenty Years at Hull House*, to wide acclaim. Convinced that women could

Jane Addams (far right) in a woman suffrage parade, around 1912

In 1915, Jane (fourth from left) sailed to the Netherlands to attend the International Women's Peace Conference.

change the world if given a political voice, she campaigned for women to be allowed to vote.

In 1914, a devastating war erupted across the Atlantic. Hundreds of thousands of young men were dying on the battlefields of France, Italy, and eastern Europe. In 1915, Jane Addams joined women from warring and neutral nations at the International Women's Peace Conference in the Netherlands. While their sons and husbands were shooting one another from the trenches, the women called for the founding of a permanent international court that could resolve disputes between nations without bloodshed.

With a burst of patriotic zeal, the United States entered World War I in 1917. While bands played

In 1917, at a time when most Americans were cheering on troops departing for World War I battlegrounds (left), Jane Addams remained committed to her plea for peace.

and America's young men put on khaki uniforms, Jane Addams continued her plea for peace. Even some of her closest friends turned away from her, aghast at her refusal to support her country. But Jane felt that all wars were morally wrong. Later she admitted, "I experienced a sense of social opprobrium [disgrace] and widespread misunderstanding which brought me very near to self-pity." Yet, despite vicious criticism, she held firmly to her beliefs.

When the war was over at last, Jane returned

to Europe. She visited devastated battlegrounds, comforted those who had lost loved ones, and helped distribute food to the starving. She worked just as hard helping the defeated German people as she did aiding the French and other American allies.

In the early days of Hull House, most Americans viewed Jane Addams as a saint, a blessing to the poor and downtrodden. By the 1920s, however, public opinion had turned sharply against her. She was accused of fraternizing with the enemy, and befriending those who wanted to overthrow the government. One magazine condemned Jane Addams as "the most dangerous woman in America."

However, even at the lowest point in her long career, Jane still had many faithful friends. In 1927, a group of her loyal supporters held a testimonial dinner in her honor. President Calvin

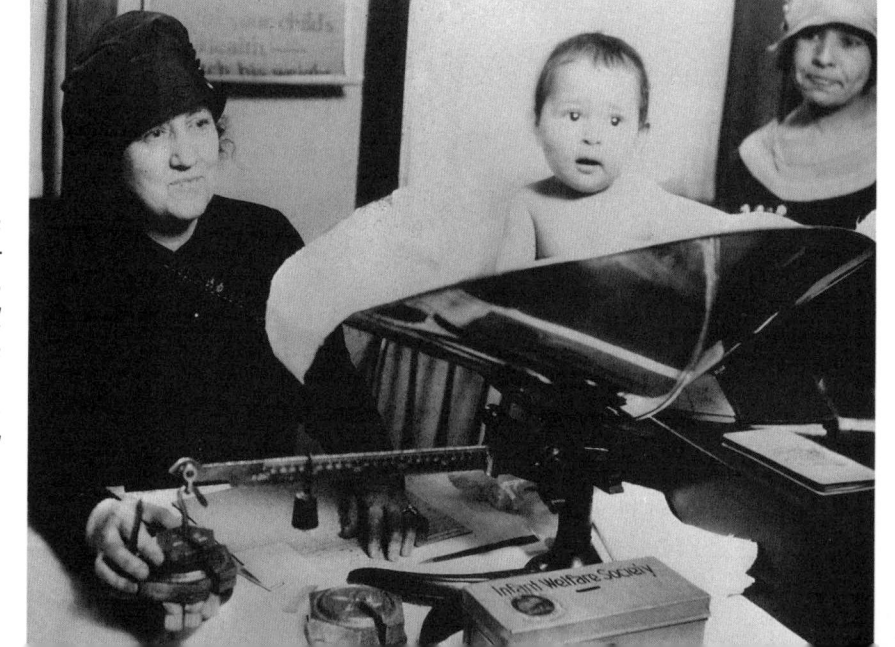

Even while Jane turned her attention to fostering world peace, Hull House continued to grow. By 1930, its services included an infant-care center.

In 1927, Jane Addams's loyal supporters held a dinner in her honor.

Coolidge sent his greetings. A telegram from New York governor Al Smith said: "In honoring Jane Addams we honor the idealism of American womanhood."

Slowly, the bitterness of the war years faded away. Some people even admitted that in speaking out for peace, Jane may have been right after all. In 1931, Jane Addams was awarded the Nobel Peace Prize, one of the greatest honors ever bestowed on an American woman. She donated the prize money—$16,480—to the Women's International League for Peace and Freedom. Prize money from two other awards

Al Smith

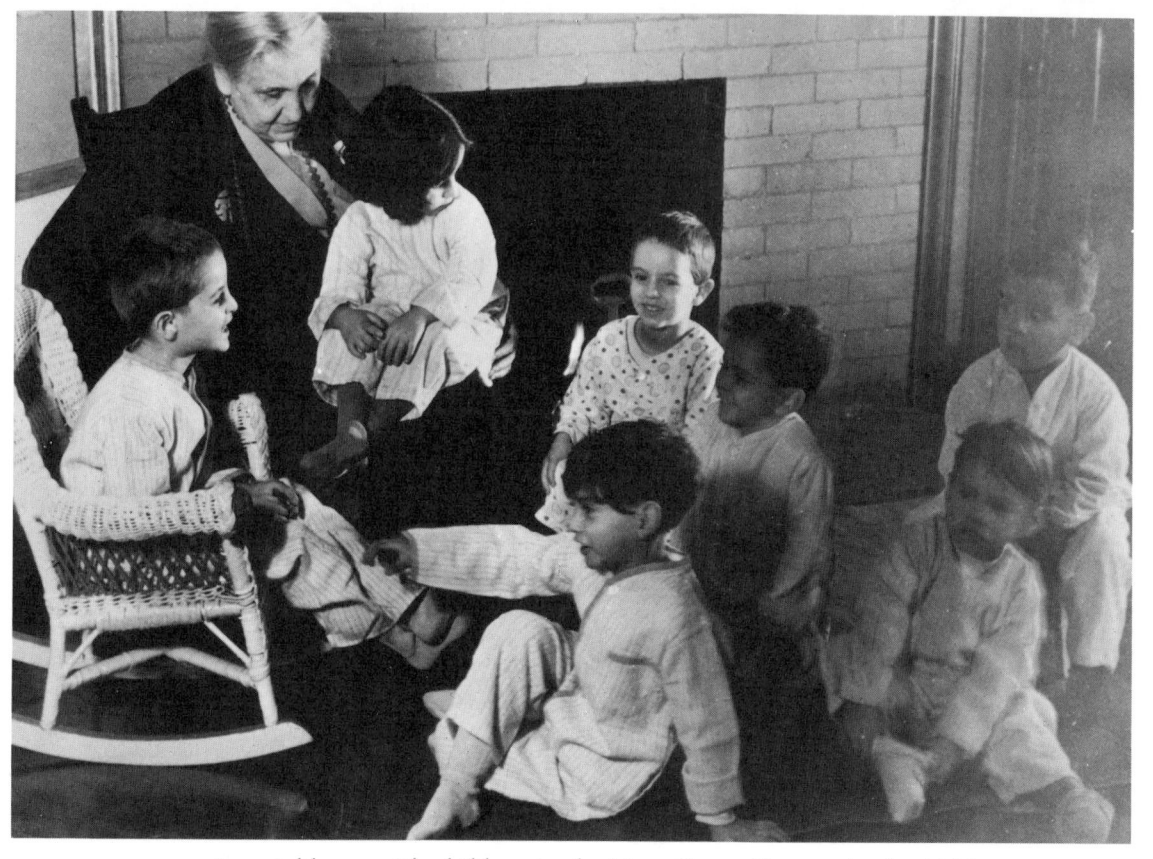

Jane Addams with children in the Mary Crane Nursery in the 1930s

she received that same year went to help the unemployed of Chicago's slums.

Busy as she was, Jane Addams still handled the finances of Hull House on her own. Most of the area's Italian and Russian families had moved to more prosperous neighborhoods. But other newcomers took their place in the tenements— including immigrants from Mexico and African Americans from the rural South. Hull House still had plenty of work to do.

Despite failing health, Jane now spent little time in Chicago. Her work with the peace movement consumed her. In speech after speech, she urged her listeners to turn inward to seek spiritual strength that would heal the world's wounds.

Dr. Alice Hamilton, who had dedicated her life to caring for the poor, stayed close to Jane Addams during her travels. Jane's health continued to decline. Stricken with cancer, she died in Chicago on May 21, 1935.

Thousands of friends and admirers filed past the coffin that stood in the reception room at Hull House. Newspapers printed impassioned

Jane Addams's funeral, Hull House courtyard, 1935

Today, the original Hull House mansion is preserved as a museum.

eulogies. Jane Addams was buried in Cedarville, Illinois, where she had spent her happy childhood.

During the 1960s, the work of the Hull House Association spread from the original settlement to some twenty locations scattered throughout Chicago's most impoverished neighborhoods. Though much of the complex on Halsted Street has been torn down, two of the original buildings remain, today surrounded by the campus of the University of Illinois at Chicago. In 1967, the Hull House mansion was opened to the public as a museum. Its collection of newspaper clippings, photographs, and films document the dedication of Jane Addams and the hundreds of men and women who helped her carry out her work.

In the years after her death, journalists, educators, and scholars paid tribute to Jane Addams. Perhaps no one expressed the meaning of her life and work more eloquently than columnist Walter Lippman: "She had compassion without condescension, and pity without retreat into vulgarity," he wrote. "She had infinite sympathy for common things without forgetfulness of those that are uncommon. That, I think, is why those who have known her say that she was not only good, but great."

Jane Addams and a young friend in the 1890s

INDEX

PHOTO CREDITS

Cover, AP/Wide World; 1, 2, 3, 4, 5 (both photos), University of Illinois at Chicago, The University Library, Jane Addams Memorial Collection; 7, North Wind; 8 (left), University of Illinois at Chicago, The University Library, Jane Addams Memorial Collection; 8 (right), North Wind; 9, 10, University of Illinois at Chicago, The University Library, Jane Addams Memorial Collection; 11 (left), North Wind; 11 (right), 12, University of Illinois at Chicago, The University Library, Jane Addams Memorial Collection; 13, North Wind; 14, University of Illinois at Chicago, The University Library, Jane Addams Memorial Collection; 15, North Wind; 16 (both photos), 17, 18, 19 (all three photos), 20, 21, University of Illinois at Chicago, The University Library, Jane Addams Memorial Collection; 22, The Bettmann Archive; 23, 24, University of Illinois at Chicago, The University Library, Jane Addams Memorial Collection; 25 Culver Pictures, Inc.; 26, 27 (top), University of Illinois at Chicago, The University Library, Jane Addams Memorial Collection; 27 (bottom), AP/Wide World; 28, 29, University of Illinois at Chicago, The University Library, Jane Addams Memorial Collection; 30, Historical Pictures Service, Chicago; 31, University of Illinois at Chicago, The University Library, Jane Addams Memorial Collection

Picture Identifications:
Cover: Jane Addams talking to Hull House neighborhood children
Page 1: Jane Addams at about the age of twenty-three
Page 2: Neighbors being greeted at the Hull House entrance, about 1913

Project Editor: Shari Joffe
Designer: Karen Yops
Cornerstones of Freedom Logo: David Cunningham

ABOUT THE AUTHOR

Deborah Kent grew up in Little Falls, New Jersey, and received her B.A. from Oberlin College. She earned a master's degree in social work from Smith College, and worked for four years at the University Settlement House on New York's Lower East Side. University Settlement, though less well-known, actually predates Hull House by two years.

Ms. Kent left social work to begin a career in writing. She published her first novel, *Belonging*, while living in San Miguel de Allende, Mexico. She has written a dozen novels for young adults, as well as numerous nonfiction titles for children. She lives in Chicago with her husband and their daughter Janna.